# The Words I Spoke

## ALAN HINES

www.trafford.com
North America & international
toll-free: 1 888 232 4444 (USA & Canada)
fax: 812 355 4082

Books of poetry already published by Alan Hines,
1. Reflections of Love
2. Thug Poetry Volume 1

Urban Novel already published by Alan Hines,
1. Book Writer

Upcoming books of poetry by Alan Hines,
1. Reflections of Love (Volume 2,and 3)
2. This is Love (Volume 1, 2, and 3)
3. Founded Love (Volume 1,2, and 3)
4. True Love (Volume 1,2,and 3)
5. Thug Poetry (Endless Volumes)
6. When Thugs Cry (Volume 1,2,and 3)
7. A Inner Soul That Cried (Volume 1,2,and 3)
8. Visionary (Endless Volumes)
9. In My Eyes To See (Volume 1,2, and 3)
10. A Seed That Grew (Volume 1,2,and, 3)
11. The Words I Spoke (Volume 1,2 and 3)
12. Scriptures (Volume 1,2, and 3)
13. Revelations (volume 1,2, and 3)
14. Destiny (Volume 1,2, and 3)
15. Trials and Tribulations (Volume 1,2, and 3)
16. IMMORTALITY (Volume 1,2, and 3)
17. My Low Spoken Words (Volume 1,2, and 3)
18. Beauty Within (Volume 1,2, and 3)
19. Red Ink of Blood (Volume 1,2, and 3)
20. Destiny of Light (Jean Hines) (Volume 1,2, and 3)

Upcoming non-fiction books by Alan Hines,
1. Time Versus Life
2. Timeless Jewels
3. The Essence of Time

Upcoming Urban Novels by Alan Hines,
1. Queens of Queens
2. Black Kings
3. Playerlistic
4. The Police
5. Scandalous
6. The West Side Rapist
7. Shattered Dreams
8. She Wrote Murder
9. Black Fonz
10. A Slow Form of Suicide
11. No-Love
12. War Stories
13. Storm
14. Ghetto Heros
15. Boss Pimps
16. Adolescents
17. In The Hearts of Men

# *Acknowledgements*

As always it's special thanks to the creator up above for blessing me in each and every way. Special thanks to my grandmother Jean Hines, whom are in Heaven; Without you being brought to life their could never be me. I love you, and always thinking of you. Special thanks to my mom, and dad without them from God I wouldn't even exist. Special thanks to my sister Alicia for being there for me in most worsest times of need, and for giving me the idea to become an author. Special thanks to Julie Hull (attorney), John Fitzgerald Lyke (attorney), and to Mr. Marasa (English Teacher). Special thanks to anybody else that showed me any love, and support throughout life.

Thanks to the entire Hines, and Laughlin family, all my co-workers. Thanks to everybody that's always asking when my next book is coming out. Thanks Ricardo Sanchez, for being there in a time when I needed you most. Roscell Hines(Cel), Alan White(Block), Shamon Miller(Pac), everyday I pray that liberty, everlasting freedom, and happiness will all come together as one sooner, then later.

Thanks to any and everybody that will decide to read this book, and I hope everybody enjoys it.

# 1. Listen

In addition never graduated, didn't listen to the ministers intuition which was to be in a powerful position.

To be a misses instead of a mistress.

Be observant, and do your own surveys, and general statistics.

Yet and still she didn't listen as he told her education was the key to success within

existence, to study King James version limited edition.

Once she got older she sat reminiscing, all five of kidsfathers missing.

Public housing living, check to check living.

Doing strange things to feed her, and her children.

Now she wish she would've listen, while the minister was telling her of premonitions.

# 2. Dignity and Pride

She had a good sense of pride that wouldn't let her inner soul cry, or die.

Felt as she could extend her arms to reach the sky.

Never questioning why.

Couldn't feel the heat from fire, soothing inside.

Champion of mountains she'd climb.

A leader with followers always by her side.

Held her head up high as she glide.

Would never accept a prize could see angels in her eyes.

On her day of birth she was baptized, worship God with dignity and pride.

# 3. A Different Time

A different time, a zone, a frame of mind.
A new world order was design.
Enemies leading ally troops from behind to the blind.
Addicted substances controlled minds.
Reenacting the massacre of St. Valentines.
Pedophiles in grammer school lines.
Bootlegging liquor turned back to a crime.
Boston taxes on tea recently inclined.
Living hundreds of years in lifetimes before dying as B.C. times.....
A different time.

# 4. Jesus Christ

I know he died for our sins.
If time repeats itself I know he'd do it again.

His blood lies in the heart of men.

No creature on earth could cast the first stone, because we all have sinned,

some will even do it again.

The son of men.

He died for our sins.

# 5. A Shaded True of Knowledge

She sat under this shaded tree, couldn't see the entire truth of knowledge,

this tree shaded her from problems, the dimness of the sun only shined a bit of the truth of knowledge.

She couldn't see upcoming conditions that wouldn't be so marvelous.

Crying babies with no fathers.

Venereal diseases that had no cure for regardless.

Those content with receiving W.I.C. and section 8 apartments.

In summers women half dressed wearing garments.

Those with problems mainly because they didn't make wise decisions regardless.


Her future couldn't be prosperous because she sat under the shaded tree that shaded her from the truth of knowledge.

# 6. Count From One Through Ten

1. **O**ne is for the people that create problems as a sequel, evil. 2. Two is for those fools that dropped out of school, disregarding knowledge as a

powerful tool.

3. Three is for those that didn't even attempt to experience life, and better things to see.

4. Four is for those that wasn't focused to walk through opened prosperous doors.

5. Five was for those that used, misused drugs O.D. and died.

6. Six, six is for gang members that showed false love to a sense had minds playing tricks.

7. Seven is for those that were slayed for sins they shall see hell instead of heaven.

8. Eight is for those with natural life, and shall never exit the prisons gate.

9. Nine is for those constant standing in dope lines, little kids getting killed dying, while the pastor profits off lying.

10.Ten is for those that did a stretch, ten or fifteen within, got out and start selling dope again....count from one through ten.

# 7. Continue

I'll continue to tell you what's on the menu.

There's been a change of venue.

Jobs that will suspend you.

Friends with no helping hands, no money to lend you.

Some never been where I been, do what I do.

Terminal illness that will effect those as easy as the flu.

No more red, white, and blue.

Wild animals break up outta the Zoos.

Confused not knowing where to go or what to do.

Words that will definitely offend you.

False instead of true.

Not even having a clue.

Doing you, but listen to me as I'll continue to tell you what's on the menu.....

# 8. Controlled Fates

Controlled all fates.
Demonic demons being pushed and kicked out of heavens gates.

The evil that body and souls do theirs no escape.

Violence some can't wait.

Setting dates for crimes of hate to take place;

burning of crosses to this day.

White sheets took away but in hearts racism shall forever stay.

The lake of fire where adolescents souls shall forever lay for the committed offenses

against God's scriptures he created.

Easy used devil's bait, deniros, and pornography on first date.

Stuck in prison, once a month state pays.

Awaiting on appeals, and outdates, and some will forever stay until death take them

away.

Lucifer paved the way, having things his way, and contolloing fates.

# 9. Engulf

E ngulfed in flames.
Yelling of insanity using Jesus Christ name in vain.
Insanes playing mind games.
Trouble came, lions preyed on human beings.
Constant bodies being slain.
Militant devil worshipping gangs, that love to gangbang.....
Imagine being engulfed in gasoline then in flames.

# 10. Breadwinner

A breadwinner that's one of the many reasons I made her my bottom.

Met her on one of the sensational days in autumn.

She read all my books of poetry and I said I was heaven sent, a prophet.

Little did she know I felt the opposite, to me she was inspirational,

marvelous, helpful with knowledge.

Smarter than those with those P.H.D's in college.

Loved me regardless.

She knew how to make an honest prophet.

A breadwinner my bottom.

# 11. Never Hopeless

N ever Hopeless, concentration,
never losing focus.

The one that wrote a magical hocus pocus.

Like a friendly ghost.

Traveling coast to coast.

Striving for most.

A celebrated toast.

An everyday party host.

Stuck in a match on the ropes, but once off the ropes,

winnings and accomplishments shall overload.

Keeping the faith within hope.

# 12. Darkside

A darkside where 24hrs. a day 7 days a week there was no light outside.

Both teams didn't coincide.

No love for the other side.

They were murdering and getting killed no one naturally died.

You could ride pass and look to see the flaming fires of wickedness in eyes, those that hated and despised.

Like Vampires thirsty to see blood, and take away lives.

Laugh out loud at funerals, no cries.

Separated family ties.

As God children were killed didn't naturally die.

Lucifer's legacy inclined.

Gave Lucifer a new life in which he didn't seek or find.

It came through crime.

Still alive.

The darkside.....

# 13. In Vain

Visualizing those that tried to put me to shame, cause me pain, using my name in vain.

Those addicted to heroin and crack cocaine.

Eternal fire on earth as it flames.

Screaming demons giving birth to men.

Acid being poured on skin.

Bit by those I loved and considered as family and friends.

German Shepherds that eat away at my flesh then within.

Crying inside to finally meet a true friend.

Flashing faces of those that plotted against me in sin.

Behind my back with knives ready to dig in.

In vain they used my name and will do it again.

# 14. Views

Went out amongst protestors to voice her political views.
Nurtured children that had been abused.

Alcohol, tobacco, and drugs she never used.

Convinced drop outs to get back in school.

Used the King James bible and Qur'an as a tool.

She was super smooth, felt as if loyalty ruled.

Those that had issues she walk in their shoes,

giving advice on how to take away the rough edges and cruise.

She told people depend not on their own understanding because

God has authority over lifetime jewels.....

Through it all she went out and shared her views helping others to improve.

# 15. Mind

In the back of my mind I be internally crying wondering why people

gotta do time.

Family members, and friends steady dying, witness, witnesses testify, signs

of the devil's eternal fire, souls crying, usage of drugs as brain fries,

little kids that backslide, and masters in lying.

Funeral of crying, puddle of blood babies drown, lie, and die in.

No holy water lives of sin.

Poking knives in the hearts of men,

can't even trust my next of kin.

in the back of my mind I wonder how long will I live without dying.

# 16. Reactions

Chemical Reactions
Kidnapping
Fainting and Collapsing
Overlapsing
Backtracking
Factoring
Satisfaction
Relaxing
Cause and effect of reactions.

# 17. Based

I t was based on real life events.
Was never a real friend, bit my right hand and let
venom poison flow end.
I always wondered where your time and
money was being spent;
you was going against.
Covered up your real intent,
you did a good job to pretend.
You had ill intentions to begin,
in the center within you schemed from my Bejamin Franklin's skin,
literally stabbed me in the back in the end.


I should've paid more attention to the obvious sins of men.
Besides I met you over a state tray while I resided in the belly of the
beast within.

# 18. Tendecies

Murdering tendecies.
Never committed any crimes but
life long felonies he'd loved it to see.
Fantasies of misery, and loved company.
Mental attitude of burns, third degree.

Happily married.
Went to church every week, but still allowed demonic spirits to be free.
No one on earth can live perfectly.

Gave him a badge,
pass the police academy.
In the line of duty killed a thirteen year old in the streets falsely,
and then a second badge of honor and promotion he received.

# 19. Poetic Lines

P oetic lines, love and happiness combined.
A stimulant for minds.

Love at it's prime.

The best of it's kind.

Space age, that of another time.

Words that coincide as ryhmes, a freed mind.

Alphabets that come together and grind to enhance clues and visions in minds.

Reading, writing and reciting poetry lines.

# 20. Disguised Blessings

Bad experiences, and painful learned lessons in reality was disguised blessings.

Learned how to cherish gifts, and value sessions.

Repass of past aggressions brought forth smiles without questions.

Loving opposites genders presence.

Genuinely giving without expecting back commandments,

never forgot when I didn't have it.

Never went back as freedom became everlasting.

# 21. Just Remembered

They was gone through october, november
and all through september.
No love in the coldest of winters.
When it was no heat, cold air through cracks in walls,
and windows.
A genuine friend a sacred place of rememberence
I don't remember.
But I just remembered sick grown men molested children.
Project living.
Senseless killings.
Grade school children can't even get to school,
to much gun fire by civilians,
to many customers in lines of dealings surrounding buildings.
I just remember the chaos that suspended
through october, november, and through the rest
of the months until september.

# 22. Delicately Refined (Jean Hines)

Delicately refined, intellectual mind.

Forever placed in her prime.

She was before her time.

Spoke to people about reading the holy bible

to ease minds.

Spiritually inclined.

Read the word for those to go forward not being in the blind,

left behind of God's grace and mercy that was in

reach not hard to find.

Stayed on my behind letting me know that she loved me all the time,

and that through her teachings I shall someday shine.

Provided timeless jewels that would last a lifetime.....

I called her momma, but her name was Jean Hines.

# 23. Variation

I t be a variation of fiendish things that aint what they seem.
Survival tactics all revolved around schemes.

Living our own American dream.

In denial of certain things we've heard, done or seen.

Replica or clone is what is seen, but in reality it's the real thing.

Affiliants crowning themselves as kings,

in reality our father whom are in Heaven is the king of kings;

to get to him you must go through his sons name.

Cravings, fiending, and desiring a variation of things.....

# 24. A Rhyme, A Word

A rhyme, a word, a melody, a tempo, a poetic vibe being felt, and heard.

A mic of spoken word that came from Psalms, and Proverbs.

A vitalize of animated nerves.

Respect earned and deserve.

A love for hers.

Unconditional rhyme stirs, lost in love for the play of words.

A strategic path that sometime curves.

A rhyme, a way with words.

# 25. Contrary Beliefs

Contrary to popular beliefs.

She was more great than the Great Barrier Reef.

She was someone I just had to keep.

Was a part of me, pave the way for love to be, to see.

Kept me focusely.

Some would tell me bad things about her in deceit;

others would tell her bad things about me.

I forgot what others think I shall be with that special someone

I love whole-heartedly, complete, and feels the same way about me,

and that was she.

Contrary to popular beliefs, I loved her and she loved me.

# 26. Right Hand

My right hand is to Allah father of the universe,
my left hand is Satan Dragon of the beast.
My right hand shall crush my left hand, the beast.
As I face the east saying a prayer for those that's deceased,
those stuck in poverty, those that will never see the streets.

New laws unfold as crime didn't decrease.
Some use drugs, and pop pistols as a way,
a way of being free.

A product of their environment is what they came to be.
Nieve to power of knowledge, and education, years studying
to get a degree.
Wouldn't have to see jail cells, forever free.
Bank accounts of legitimately hard earned money,
no drug sells to see.

The serpent in hell planted bad seeds that ruined
the streets.
Death and destruction is all we see.
Kids being murdered daily.

Riots of firely burning souls,
those with no where to live, stuck in the cold.
As DCFS kids moms and dads strung out on cocaine, and blows,
controlled substances that turned out lost souls.

Violating parole in and out prisons doors.
Violent cases constant being caught as
animinalistic human beings refuse to fold,
refuse to let go of street life,
even when some grow old.
Stuck in time of dungeons and dragons in which the
beast controlled.

# 27. Pitiful

P itiful cries, could never whip away tears from eyes,
burning flames of fire,

and everyone shall be killed or die.

Hypes that steady getting high.

Sanctified saints that hold they head down praying to the sky.

Hoping one day their kids and grandkids will seek the truth

instead of living in a lie.

Praying to see Heaven in the sky after they die.

Never questioning the Lord why,

but faithfully serving him down on earth as it is

in the sky.


Pitiful cries of people that will never be baptize earthly

devils without disguise,

utilize criminal enterprise,

seeing demonic spirits in eyes.

Meeting The dragon of the beast before and after we die.

Nightmares coming to reality in lives.

No steady flow of income hustle to get by since 1965.
Still aint taking advantage of dedicating to
grow and climb.

Constant mayhem,
and pitiful crying.

# 28. Present Eyes, Future lies

C aught up in a repetition of lies,
    where scandalous ones come with surprise,
kidnapping, torchering, to die.
Saints often ask why?
Why must these people achieve a rush a rise off sick crimes,
never stopping as they get worser each time.
Causing insanity in minds.
Saints constantly visioning burning of mankind,
Satan inclined.
Those being set out and rotten like a fruit or vine.
Came to find, that the Myans was lying the earth didn't
come to end at that date, and time, but people steady dying,
revolutionary, revelation times;
the bible was the truth as state attorney's getting convictions
off lying.
But in time God's true followers shall see the bright light
that shall ever shine.
Outta the dark comes the light of lime.

Earthly bodies shall frequently see the dark within their life

time, but after death dark alleys, or night time doesn't exist

in Heaven's enterprise.

Heavenly souls cannot begin dying,

life has just begin as an everlasting light shine forever

blessed with eternal life without dying,

those that followed faithfully and didn't stay behind;

shall bare witness to the paradise that lies.....

Present Eyes, Future Lies.

# 29. Love and Respect

With me it's all about love, and respect.

Showing love, dispite of, to never forget.

Wanting and needing, never let.

Being there when times are worst or best.

No change of wearing sides of hats.

I'm with, those that are against, reject, protest, and don't rotate with.

The ones I know break bread with.

Not the ones that was fake, and pretend;

true colors came out of what had always been within.

Love, loyalty, and respect is a built within me as a men until the very end.

# 30. Silent Mind

S ometimes in my silent mind I feel peace as those that had won The Nobel Peace Prize.

Others times I feel like a horror story that came alive.

Sometimes I be watching her from behind thinking of the right words

to get her to be mines, to see what's underneath the fabric designs.

Sometimes I be wanna write love poems that ryhme;

other times I be wanna write fiction about a killer that lost his mind.

Sometimes I take memorable drifts through my own mind, back to the future, present day in time, or futuristic optimist prime.....

Some try to read me and draw off signs, but you don't what's going on in my silent mind.

# 31. Cry Baby

Never ending impending sounds of crying babies.
Daddies maybes, driving me crazy.
Lord please save me, from the madness, chaos,
and screaming of being raped ladies.
Crack fiend mother's giving birth to crack babies.
Crying, screaming, driving me crazy.
Where's your sitter baby?
There's love unconditionally from me daily.
Milk and pampers wont phase me.
Just please stop crying baby.
It's a whole world out there, God made for you and me.
You got you whole life ahead to live to see.
The creator got a plan for you and me.
Things that's destine to be.....
Stop crying baby, and let things be what they be.

# 32. A Day of Birth

A day of birth from my fair lady that was from Heavens, but reside on earth.

Made my feel the goodness of living life for what it's worth,

and the loving embrace that emerged.

Her mere words were calmness of nerves, felt as if I was soaring with birds.

She was like a sensational straight path with no curves.

Gave me all her love she felt I deserve.

A melodramatic dream come true to be hers.....


A day of birth from my fair lady that was from the Heavens,

but resided on Earth.

# 33. A Bloody Rage

A bloody rage, memories fade.
Innocent kids were slayed,

now resting in graves,

struck by strays.

Will never again see the light of days.

No suspect the killers got away.

Some walk, talk and live this way.

Survival tactics of men in caves.

The tricks, and the games people play especially to get paid.

Leading, and being led astray.

Booster's that can't keep their hands away.

Killers that take away lives feeling no remorse, no dismay.

To some it's just an ordinary day.

# 34. Timeless Times

At times life gets hard yet and still I kept my faith in God. knowing his son blood shed played a part.

I walk the streets in the dark gazing at the stars visualizing

life beyond mars.

Spaceships no cars.

Feeling sad for those that got life behind bars.

Wishing upon a freedom star to follow where you are.

I'm yearning to live life large, and of other life's be a divine part.

# 35. Excited

Excited me delighted me.
Inspired me to write poetry, endlessly a friend, to me,
gave me her own eyes so I could see.
So I could be me free.....
For I am her and she is me; excited me.

# 36. Existence

It does exist, white sheets were traded, for badges, and guns, and law degrees.

It does exist a Christmas with no presents, or even trees.

Most are screaming, and crying for blessings.

Those we go to for confesssions are pedophiles,

homosexual child molesters.

It does exist H.I.V. infected infants from breast feeding.

Slow down take heed to the existing things amongst thee.

# 37. Confinements

I rritating confinements.
Immigrants crossing the scrimmage linings.

To Allah, Jehovah, and God for freedom prisoners are crying.

Bleached eyes being blinded.

Worrying of uncontrollable past state of minding.

Madness is there never had to find it.

Never accept a free lunch, people wanting something in return for kindness.

With a full grown monkey on your back, chasing a dragon of dreams

within controlled substances addictional confinements.....

Let us free, from confinements.

# 38. Changed My Silence

Changed my silence the words I spoke
were that of love at it's finest,
like unleashing a precious jewel, diamond.
Some knowledge was indirect, and others was direct
in the right place in timing.
Gave keys to smartness of masterminding,
doing things in the right place in time,
as currency inclined.
Making love to a woman's heart, and mind, now
our bodies entwine.
Changed my silence giving people a piece of my mind
hoping my experiences and knowledge can help them within
their lifetime.

# 39. Philosopher

This ancient Greek philosopher once said,
"evil minds in time."
He meant, evil minds shall entertwine forever in time.
Criminal elements assortments of crimes of all kinds.
Wickedness design.
Co-defendants in trial going against testifying.
Parents somewhere shopping in drug lines,
while new borns left at home alone continuously crying.
Alot of people not trying to grow in time.
A content mental state of being in welfare lines.
Street thugs with militia men military minds.
Those that love scandals, and lies.
Convicted felons who keep the same frame of mind throughout lifetimes.
Past decades aggression, and crimes revolved to today's minds.....
Evil minds think a like in time.

# 40. Conquered

Conquered Great Britian, England and even Spain.
In thundering rain war without peace became.

Lion hearted war games.

Soilders war changed, as opponents cheered in lanes.

General titles were gained.

As blood became permanent stains.

Mind frames were rearranged.

Those that was good now possessed hearts of flame.

But they still used their brain.

Unloading them things, breaking the sound barrier within war games.

At the end of everything we conquered Great Britian, England, and Spain.

# 41. My only friend

God is my only true friend snatched away from that life of sin.
A terrific hero to men.

Where was everybody else when I only needed short sums for someone to lend,

a helping hand, there was no women or men.

But God continue to give a shoulder to lean, my destiny he made through his

vision was seen.

My king of kings praise thy holy name.

I love all the things you bring even the sun, and the rain,

the sweetness of sugar cane.

The wonders of what life brings.

Having my five senses, able to touch, smell, taste, hear,

and see things; thanks to my king of kings.


I must admit I haven't been to church in a while,

but yet and still I love being one of your golden childs.

# 42. Mere Glimpse

A mere glimpse of reality.
Finish college, still can't find a decent salary.
Exercising to burn calories;
surgeon general report says everything is a health formality.
Dead beat dads not interested in feeding families.
Diseases spread timely.
No options or probability, mere glimpse of reality.

# 43. Tears of A Man

Tears of a lost man.
Dying mold.

Scrolls of black souls.

Stories unfold.

The truth was told.

Those that we ran with was the snakes, dressed up in human skin wearing the finest clothes.

Those that you helped was the ones that stole your role.

Those you loved, and consoled in the end was the ones that went behind your back,

and told.


Tears of a lost man.

Undying mold.

## 44. Better or Worse

For better or worse I'll choice you first.
   Richer turned poor I love you more.
Sickness or good health my love shall always be felt.
Sun or ran the joy of love I shall always bring to my queen.

# 45. Again and Again

He keep doing it again, committing treason against ally arm forces and friends.

Filled with wanting revenge.

Screaming and cursing with no end.

Fire and gasoline blended in.

Heart burn with no end of wanting sin.

Again, and again he did felonious capers not to fit in,

but because it made him feel like a giant within.

He did it again, and again, my evil twin.

# 46. Identity Crisis

Indentity crisis, no social security
number and lost my license.
Secretly I lived in silence.
Not knowing my history or future blindly.
Confused, idoly.

Indentity crisis without a team.
Don't understand no one or what anything means.
Living a lie through a dream.

My indentity was a fiction story written as a scheme.

# 47. Herself

You can tell by the way she carried herself that
she dieted well stayed in the best of health, and took care of
herself.

She stayed to herself as a way to find her inner self.

She'd write poetry and her lyrical words were being felt.

By herself pleasure was being dealt.

In war soilders were killed,

bad hands were being dealt,

natural causes of heart attacks were real,

but she remained tranquil in her heart love was filled.

A virgin from birth, death until.

Followed the King James version for real, non-hypocritical.

Yet and still more deadly than blue steel in her poetic deal.

Writing poetry people could feel.

# 48. Came and went

S he came and went.
  Trillions pennies of cents.
Potpourri scent.

Had my nose open.
Had me praying, and hoping.
Smoothly coasting, overdose, surfing her ocean.
In swimsuit positons she posed in.
She never supposed, only for me she never kept her legs closed.
A revolving door, always wanting more.

She came and went like the re-election of presidents.
Had my eyes low, and bent.
Started as a friend, turned into a gem.
Her name was Kim.

I showed her it's greater in the end.

She came and went.

Before long she came, stayed concluded went,

because I treated her as a wife of a prince.

# 49. Sin

Hideous intentions,
blood shed and convictions.

Demonic premonitions.

Dead bodies that sleep with fishes.

Angels of death blowing kisses.

Arabians on suicide missions.

Plastic surgeons that cut with precisions.

Unmarked faces that commit deadly sins again, and again.

My only childhood friend was raped and killed by

her next of kin when she was only ten.

Muslims that get sick from eating the pigs skin,

showing no respect for the Koran,

or the crescent moon of the fin.

As the Judicial system leave people within.

Religious men that drown in there own sin.

Dark nights as evil begins with no end.

Lucifer followers, follows his commandments.

Vampires that shoot up blood through a dirty syringe.

No friends.

No abortions, kids being born orphans.

Politicians being extorted.

Goverment plans that will never be affording.

Homicidal harmonizing melodies play from accordions.

Everyone's mentality on one accord being evil which

was implanted through umbilical cords.....

These sins of you, and yours.

# 50. Please Never Leave

I sit manifesting these words.
Hoping my love for you through poetry will be heard.

In the morning I wake up to the chirping of birds,
as your vision ease my nerves,
give my life the meaning it deserves.

For you I breathe the air I breathe.
You're like a summer's day with air blowing through trees.
My life please never leave.
For my love unto to you take heed.
Knowledge as nourishments you feed.

A personal stripper that tease.....
Please never leave.

# 51. Contemporary Arts

Contemporary arts.
Signs of the light and the dark,
falling angels that unite hearts.
Fireworks that's celebrated through sparks.
Dead artist bring to life art.
A place beyond the stars contemporary
parts of art.

# 52. Writings

I became addicted to my writings actually
seeing UFO sightings.
Remembering the Titans.
Pit Bulls that was fighting.
A delighting.
Poetry writing and reciting with all my will, and might.
To those I love keeping it tight.
Day and night I'm addicted to write.

# 53. Laced

A lovely taste.
Warm embrace.
Passionant laced.
The cutest face.
Memories couldn't never be erased.
Forever stay; without a route for escape.
The sweetest, loveliest of a lovely taste, laced.

# 54. Arouse

Arouse.
Unfold a red rose that control souls,
opened up doors to show floors that love will continuously grow.
An alarming flow.

Arouse from the oceans floor to stay afloat.
Safety as a net or rope.

Arouse to see what life has in store.

# 55. Thundering Rain

Thundering rain.
  Pleasure and pain.
Saying names.
Coming and came.
Bodily fluids being exchange.
Baby showers shall be arranged.....
Happiness gained in the midst of thundering rain.

# 56. Painted Portraits

S he painted portraits of Ancient Egyptians
that held down fortress.
Indians that attached ships of Christopher Columbus.
Africans that put the white men in bondage.
Bank tellers that held robbers hostage.
Poor now living marvelous.

She painted portraits of people living the fullest
of life without problems.
How this earth revolved.

She painted portraits of the way she felt past history,
and how today's current date should be.

# 57. A Great

A master in debating.
Self-educated, graduated.

All in love, those that dated.

Others smartness conquered and overrated.

No duplicate, can't be imitated.

Wanted to soar the world to see what was awaiting.

Actor of plays.

Recited spoken words on stage.

During debates the audience listen to what ones had to say.

An expert in thinking, and knew how to debate.

# 58. Loving Sequel

Maybe this time we will take it slow, giving our love time to grow.

Letting others that try to come between flow.

She really love me so, and the feeling is mutual.

This time we gotta take slow filling the gaps, blanks, and holes.

More interested in others need for love to grow.

She soared in the air like an eagle.

Yet, and still her and I were ordinary people.

Loving with a sequel.

# 59. Bad Wishes

Wishes, factitous suspicious,
  phony kicking it, Lucifer's intuition.
Poking of flesh with knives from kitchens.
No concerns or affectional decisions.
Stuck in a three d spaced out dimension.
No one to listen.
Drowning in own blood from sick wishes.
Individuals hoping you come up missing.
Achieving spiteful wishes to create fragmental incisions.
Devilish and Satanic collisions.
Anarchy across the globe we live in.....
The beast within.

# 60. It's Strange

I t was strange how things became.
Sitting across from her she'd watch me silently
whispering my name.
To her I was the Godd of rain;
moisture came to her heart and brain, letting her live again.

It's strange how she'd watch me and long
to play love games.
She wanted me to tap into her brain.
Hypnotize to the happiness I could bring.
All day, each day she wanted us to connect
so pregnancy could be arranged.

Famously fame.
Preaching in a poetic mind frame.
Loving that would never change.

Life long fantasies were exchange; doing anything,
as body parts stiffen and sometimes hang.

It's strange how at first I didn't even know her name.
Now, her and I are king, and queen.

# 61. Strip

S trip me lock me in a cage on stage, blindfold my eyes on that date.

Listen to me as I go into rage visualize Lesbian slaying male gays,

poking out eyes for blood to waste.

Villages and towns being burned as people run away through a maze.

Living life running in a phase.

All dark nights with no days.

Petrafying words I'll convey.

Rapist themselves being raped.

No such things as holidays.

It's just me blind on stage as hardcore poetry is being conveyed.

Leave me in this cage so I can tell you my vision in a poetic rage.

# 62. She Is Me, Jean Hines

For she gives me, she gave me.
  Open my eyes to see,
guides my spiritually.
In her good visions is all I see.
Always been there for me.
The loveliest angel it could ever be.
For I am her, and she is me.

# 63. Medieval

From medieval times where wicked witches and evil spirits controlled minds.

Up until today's date, there are those that don't mind killing, don't mind dying.

Early teens stand in line, young dope fiends, dope they buying.

On the flip side of crime, those from the streets themselves on stands in state, and federal courts testifying.

Informants, snakes that ate every rat play each time.

In the back of minds knowing that they'll never cross the threshold were thoroughbred and the real ones reside.

Blind of the world from front and behind.

Stuck in a life of undying crimes.....

Medieval Times.

# 64. Inner Screams

Hollering, screaming, yelling,
crucifying, and telling.
Living and dying, an institutionalize felon.
Go against the law rebillion.
Killing after killing.
Parents being killed by their own children.
Internal bleeding, of no healing.

Inner screams that crack glass, windows, and
falling ceilings.

# 65. Time and Span

T ime and span.
No time for those that pretend.
No phonyness to contend.
I shall live like a man.
Avoiding fake friends.
Working hard for dividends.
Planning for the future.
Striving for the best in the end.
Time span.

# 66. Perceptions of The Devil

Perceptions of the Devil.
Streets burn on fire on each and every level.
Children born and grow up in the poverty of the ghetto.
Addicts use drugs and will never let go.
Aid checks spent on guns and ammo.
Devil is in the form of flesh of each
one you know.
Those whom have not sin shall cast the first stone.
Look in the mirror, and there you go, perceptions of the Devil.

# 67. On The Road

On the road again, going places that I've already been.
Within a journey that will never end.
On the road again as I'm a hitchhiker picked up by a psychic.
As I drove on this road the psychic tells me stories I already know, and tells me
stories I personally wrote on the road.
Started to get a little sleepy, but kept my eyes open never close;
focused on the ahead roads.
Dwelling on my youth, still remember the powerful
messages that was told.
Steady digging trying to find a pot of gold.
Evading political tolls.
Feeling like a kid running away from home,
but still making decisions of being grown.
On this road the psychic continued telling the truth,
which I already know.
Wondering will I ever get off this road, and make it home.

# 68. Time To Die

Maybe, just maybe it was my time to die.
Roaming the streets living a lie.
Undetermined sentence in seg,
institutionalized, painful cries.

Maybe it is my time to die sitting in
the electrical chair to fry.
Or maybe lethal injection will account for my demise.
Maybe I shall be hung by a rope in front of the audience eyes.
Maybe the guillotine shall take away my 9 lives.

Maybe it is my time to die,
a poker face for my fear to hide.
Wondering what day my family, and friends shall
dress up in black to cry.
Once the tears dry I'll rest in peace in my time to die.

# 69. Alone

Unanswered texts, and my calls to phones.

Some fake it, but in reality they wanted me leave them alone.

Love wasn't shown.

Even as a adolescence I had to man up be mature be grown.

Really never had a place to call home.

Shellshocked from Rockwell's war zones.

Sick vomiting dope fiends keep sweating for money wont leave me alone.

Early years teenagers wont listen to parents, think they grown.

Since fourteen been on my own, now grown I'm still so gone, so alone.

# 70. The Real World

Living in the world that really does exist.
The Devil gets bliss off teenagers that smoke dipped cigarettes;
formally known as happy sticks,
that had minds playing tricks.
Fights that had always been fixed.
Kids that didn't make Santa Claus list, simply because Santa Claus
really don't exist, never did.
The world where politicians make promises that they knew they
wouldn't stick with.
Jobs only giving because everybody else quit.
Gruesome past don't want to reminisce.
Living in the world that really does exist.

# 71. Our Lady of Sorrows

Our lady of sorrows, what will my destiny be tomorrow.

Will I reach a financial peak where as I wont have to take loans to borrow.

Will I ever meet her, and possess a marriage of no letting go.

Will I be able to withstand in this world that's just so cold,

or will I get frost bite from head to toe.

Shall I live a relentless life without letting go;

or will I die young from others that create burdens, that will make me

die and suffer slow.....

Our lady of sorrows.

# 72. Mirage

S he was like a mirage a camouflage had skeletons in closets and buried bodies in the garage.

She'd miggled with stars.

In Hollywood she had won awards for being a star.

A pornagraphic star not from a far but up close and in person.

She needed no screenplay or rehearsing.

She couldn't even remember never being a virgin.

You'd see her and think she was Persian.

Innocent and pure like the springs water.

But she was more like the Devil's daughter.

Sexually and even violently she'd give out direct orders.

An immortal, animals she'd slaughter.

Those that fell in love she'd use them like a phone that was portable.

Call on them in her time of need.

Her vagina surely would feed.

Indeed she was laced with greed.

Those whom others warned didn't take heed.

Captivated by her beauty, she was a mirage and camouflage for any man's eyes to see.

She was like a suspense novel a page turner.

A female version of Ike Turner,

that created problems with a burner.

Her weapon of choice was none.

She'd use a knife or a gun.

Sold jewelry that was slum.

Wasn't interested in having fun.

Her orgasm would come from leaving bodies numb, man stun,

and heated up wickedness like her father Sa..tan.

## 73. Miracle

I believe in miracles, spiritually ritual,
realistic non-hypocritical,
loving unconditional,
visible signs and symbols,
drawing off miracles,
loving plentiful,
setting free all immigrants, and captive political prisoners.
I believe in magic the power of making things happen,
I believe in miracles.

# 74. Thou Shall

Thou shall not tell a lie.
   In the bible it says that we shall be fruitful
and multiply as I sit by watching people
getting killed as the young die.
Crack heads, and dope fiends continue to get high.
I can't lie I seen some pop pills just to get high,
just to get by, thinking they can fly high as the sky.

With these new gun laws some people still keep a gun
by their side.
They'd rather kill than die.

Persecute those that get on the stand and testify.
Why should I be confined simply because I winked my eye.
I wonder if I'll see Heaven in the sky, or burn in eternal fire.

# 75. A Moment of Silence

A moment of silence.
A minor situation permitted his anger to become a pirate.

A rage of violence, instantly happen not realizing consequential factors.

A disaster,as violence begot more violence.

Family friend shall feel the end like Myans.

Totally annihilated the man as bullets tore apart his fleshly skin;

although his life was finish revenge from his friends would be no end.

Later the one who did it was killed by the dead man's friends.

A saga continues again, again.

Friends of deceased men committed murder in the rawest form, such a deadly sin.

Over caskets ocean tears from moms, family members,and friends took dead bodies for a swim.

Lives would come to an end, but revenge, retaliation, had no end.

A moment of silence for the war against men.

# 76. Chronic Illness

C hronic illness.
Sick of seeing bums sleeping in abandon buildings,
senseless killings,
people being poor because of the unsharing of those with millions.
Racism steady popping up being revealing.
Teenage kids themselves giving birth to children.

Chronic illness.
Sick of people steady doing horrible things to inherit
wonderful feelings.
It's sad that little kids are being born infected with parents disease
and illness.
People that feel it's better to receive instead of giving.

I'm sick of feeling the pain of chronic illness but I still thank God
I'm still
living.

# 77. She Wanted Me To Sing

She wanted me to lift every voice and sing,

til the than Heaven ring, ring with the harmony of liberty.

She wanted me to set her heart, mind, and body free,

free as can be.

In bed she wanted me to be her soilder,

to be all I can be.

Stars in the skies she wanted to see.

A part of my democracy without hypocrisy she wanted to be,
be me.

She wanted us to march on to victory, but not as one,

but together her, and me.


Like a bird she wanted me to sing,

sing with the harmony of liberty letting our love be free.

# 78. Autumn

I t was a beautiful day in autumn.

A planted seed grew a rose, a caterpillar into butterfly blossomed.

Started off from rock bottom, eventually made it like the summer when it was autumn.

Never ignorant, getting goals accomplished.

All throughout the seasons of years had problems.

But worked hard regardless.

Knew that dedication would prosper.

No more struggling with financial bills,and problems, because loyalty to work the

contracts came through with advance modules on that beautiful day in Autumn.

# 79. Generation of Kids

As my reasoning for living.
I escape, and invade all ungodly systems.

For each time you talk I listen.

For kids I live and sacrifice, and die.

New born babies don't cry,

I'll whip the tears from eyes,

to tickle as laughter reside.

I love the kids endlessly with no demise.

Child molesters, and pedafilers must die and burn in the lake of eternal fire.

I love above, and beyond, and even higher.

# 80. Worldwide Maze

A worldwide maze of slave trades.
Memories that shall never fade.
Years of suffering in hearts carved, engraved.
Kidnapped through the middle passage way.
Didn't even understand the language they conveyed.
But knew it'll be no more happy holidays.
Working for free not getting paid.
Treated inhumane trying to escape from a maze.

Years later no reparation was never gave,
but instead minimum wage.

In a different way it still goes on today.

# 81. Send

S he send me swinging.
  A lifetime of dreaming.
Singing.
Hearing church bells ringing.
To, her clinging.
She defined the love meaning.
She'd send me swinging and I really mean it.

# 82. Decisions

Decisions.
Head on collisions.
Disable sight of visions.
Should've listen.
Coming up short of blessings,
and receiving what should've been giving,
simply because of bad decisions.

# 83. Meek

The meek shall inherit the Earth.
    Prosperously from birth, until the dirt.
No painful feelings, or needling from the bad nurses.
Broken curses.
Instead love being dispursed.
As a way of being free, evil spirits,
and sickning flocks of birds shall never occur.
The meek shall one day inherit the earth.

# 84. Dark Shining

B rainstorming mastermind.
  Closed his eyes like a blind man.
But knew of things past the Atlantis.
Sent Dorothy back to Kansas.
Finally told the truth that humans were actually the
past century dungeons and dragons.
Wrote self help books for students in classes.
Revoked immigration laws for Mexicans.
Religious men came to him for advice, and to tell confessions.
He was dark shining but brought forth powerful messages.

# 85. Liberist

A liberist in Liberial arts.
Shined in the dark.
Placed in hearts.
Love that would spark.
Love that would never end as it starts.
I felt so good being with this shining star.
Heard she was from a place beyond the stars.
Love that could never seperate, could never be apart.
She had the highest degree in Liberial Arts.

# 86. Sick Visions

Sickening Visions.
Children in the form of the Malitia.
Lucifers critics.
Those with talents and dreams didn't try to get it.
Over packed prisons;
lost in the system.
Sick Visions.

# 87. In Order

Doing things by the order.
Royalties by the quater.
Parents raising sons, and daughters.
Healthcare plans that's affordable.
Being everlasting, immortal.
Simplyfying to be portable.
On time, effective assistance, in order.

## 88. Free minds

Free your mind, let troubles decline stay behind.

As I'll be your tour guide to places where love and erotica combine.

Sweetest day, and Valentine's.

Making love to the body and mind.

Happily married until the end of time.

Free your mind let love be an addiction in it's prime.

Do what it takes to make a lover feel the gift of what it is to

be loved at all times.

Free your mind and let love take control of futuristic formulated times.

Free your mind.

# 89. Vibrant Vibe

She had a vibrant vibe.
   Kept hope, and brought love alive.
Stayed by my side,
even when it was a bumpy ride.
A special bound, connections, love ties.
Had me seeing things that was next in line,
open my eyes.
She never got emotional and cried, no controversy
that relied.
She had a vibrant vibe that kept hope and
our love alive.

# 90. Means

In the means that's justifiable within decisional leverages of men.
The righteousness of the hearts of men.
Wise actions, and thinking of right hands.
Letting reality stand.
Observant of things seen in a glance.
And utilize the scripture words to advance as a man.

## 91. Be

An orchestra, a symphony.
A line of poetry.
A way to be who you be.
Touching of the pianos keys.
Letting yourself be free.
And letting things be what they be.

# 92. Timeless Issues

Value spent.
Abandonment.
Those that pretend,
no new friends.
Twisted revenge.
Wishing we could all live life with no end.

# 93. Gift To Shine

Just another gift a moment in time to shine.
Loving ryhmes.

Freeing minds.

Rocks climbed.

Leaving chaos,

and madness behind.

And loving the play of words design.

# 94. 100 Poems

Didn't do anything wrong writing a hundred poems.
Love carries on in loving memory for those that's gone.
Letting my words be like a worldly clone.
Allowing veiwers to get turned on.
Some will turn to songs.
Others will share over the phone.
Others will become books, manuscripts past along.
In my own zone letting the love of poetry live on.

# 95. Manifesting Deep Thoughts

Manifesting deep thoughts.
Souls was lost.

From project windows kids were tossed.

Murder cases was caught.

Hardcore didn't know the meaning of soft.

Sexual predators stalked.

Appeals fought, and lost.

For sins they paid the cost.

Some bosses turned to workers,

as some workers turned out, and proved to be the boss.

Manifesting deep thoughts.

# 96. Mind

A peace of mind.
Trying to leave my gruesome past behind.
Once upon a time I lived a life of crime
by Lucifer's design.
Trouble was in reach always could find.
Now I exercise knowledge within minds.
Use my time to write novels, screenplays,
and poetic rhymes.
I was giving sight to my stages of being blind.
Marathon the medals be mines.
Stand triumphant in time.
The new millennium Einstein.

# 97. Praying For Better Times

Oh lord this life of mines.

I've heard a million times that if you study the word,

and serve you I'll reach the pearly gates in time.

And I pray to you, and love you all the time.

But right now I'm sick, and dying, heart soul, crying,

"ya'll working, what ya'll got nick or dimes," is what I hear all the time.

Jobs hard to find.

Substances that will ease minds, for those that sell money

shall incline, but can give you time behind.


Look in the eyes and see criminal minds that of the Devil's design.

Wonder if things will get better in due time in this life of mines.

# 98. Time, Essence

Time is of the essence, you gotta learn to appreciate blessings, less stressing.

Prepare for what's next in.

Show love to others be a friend.

Allow God to be in the hearts of men.

Timeless essence of blessed possessions.

# 99. Temptations

S ecret love making.
  Check mating.
Sub-dating.
Substance chasing.
Memory erasing.
Greed of frustrations.
Impatient lustful waiting.
Nicotine cravings.
Temptations.

# 100. Story To Tell

C rowd settle down now and listen well I gotta story to tell.

As my poets mask is unveiled.
I'll have stories to tell, and I'll tell them well.
As I raise souls from the depths of hell to recruit followers as well.
I'll tell everything that others put in fiction books to sell.
I'll tell all things society keep to themselves.

It's as opening a curtain on stage witnessing rage.
A man stabbing a woman as the murder makes the front page.
Slaying of gays.
Deaf and blind clowns on stage.
People being forced to leave their homes and live in caves,
no happy holidays.

This story I'll tell it well,
as cancer smoke is inhaled,
closet addicts revealed.

This story I'll tell will be everything I've seen,
heard, touched, taste, or smelled.....

Crowd settle down now and listen well
I got another story to tell....

Preview of upcoming book titled "Black King".

# Black Kings

# Chapter 1

I t was the middle of the night as the blue, and white police car drove swiftly up the block. The car slowed down as it reached the end of the block as the passenger examined the address of the house to make sure it was the correct address they were looking for.....

Inside the police car was two white police officer's.....

"Is the address 4955," the driver asked the passenger? "Yes it is," the passenger responded.....

The officer's parked their squad car and they bailed out of it swiftly. As they walked up the stairs before they even got a chance to ring the door bell five shots of gun fire rang out....

Two gun shots hit one of officer in the back of the head twice. The other three shots hit the other officer in the back of his head twice, and once in the neck.....

The got shots had came from across the street from the third floor of an abandon building.....

Within seconds Will, and Black was gathering up all their shit trying to swiftly exit the abandon building.....

"Hurry up," Will told Black. "Hold on I drop the banacolus," Black said.....

Once Black picked up the banacolus off the floor, they ran to the stairs, and start running down the stairs at top speed.....

They made it their car which was in front of the abandon building.....

Black made it to the drivers side of the door reached in his pocket, and couldn't find the cars keys, he panicked, and started searching all his pockets.....

"What the fuck unlock the door," Will told Black. "I can't find the keys," Black said, as he continued searching all his pockets, even the back pockets of his pants. "Look in your front pocket, the left one," Will said.

Black stuck his hand all the way in his left pocket and came up with the keys, unlocked the door got in the car reached over and unlocked the passenger side of the car. Started the car up, and got in it, and smashed off with the pedal to the metal, burning rubber.....

At top speed Black was putting forth his best effort to get away.....

"Slow down," Will said. "Slow down, we just killed two police officer's I'm trying to get away," Black said. "Man slow this car down," Will said in a demanding manner.....

Black started to slow down a little.....

"Man slow this car down, you gone get the police to start chasing us. When you do dirt like that you got to leave the scene at ease, that way the police don't get on to. I'f they see you driving fast that automatically know what it is. Now if they see you driving regular with your seat belt on blending in with the hundreds of cars passing by they are less likely to try to get at you. Even if you drive right pass them after doing dirt, as long as you're driving regular nine times out of ten they aint gonna fuck with, becuase they'll think you a regular car just driving past," Will said.....

Black slowed the car down driving at regular speed.....

They drove to a secret hide away only to stash the guns. Then they drove to another secret hide away where the usually have meetings.....

Once they made it there Will begin to think about what they just had did, and the mistakes they made.....

"You did a good job, but the way we did that was messy, we got to make it better next time. We can't slip up and drop things like we did the banacolus, and we definitely can't misplace car keys. You keep it in your mind exactly where the car keys are at. Just think if we wouldn't have found those keys we'd probably had to make it home on foot, chances are we would've been chased by the police or even caught. We would've looked real suspicious walking down the street dressed in all black carrying large equipment concealed in bags," Will said.....

"You know that no matter what happens whenever you do dirt like that you must not tell nobody not even those that's part of the Black National family," Will said.

Black remained quiet staying attentive listening to Will as Will would feed his brain powerful knowledge.....

Will, and Black were part of an organization called Black Nationals. Will was the founder of Black National, Black was the co-founder. Some may would've considered them a gang, but the Black Nationals considered themselves to be an organizations that was in existence for the upliftment of black people.

The Black Nationals was a small organiztion that consist approximately thirty members. Every once in a while they'd accept a new member. Only in meetings they'd wear all black. They did a little protesting, and preaching in schools, and churches. But mainly they focus on trying to get blacks education, on a higher level of higher learning so that blacks would be successful on a positive note. When they did their protesting, and preaching the didn't represent Black National, they represented for the black people. Black National was like a secret society.

The Black Nation was against crime, and any usage of drugs, alcohol, and tobacco usage. The only crimes that the Black nationals was up with was violent hate crimes against white people.....

The next day after they killed them two police Black Nationals held a meeting in one of the members basement that was made up like a church. Will led the meeting as usual.....

"It's about the growth, and developement of the black community. We are black, and beautiful, black beauty's. It's time for change, and improvement, and we must do what it takes to change, and improve. We were once kings, and queens we ruled the place we once lived in before the white devils came in. We governed, and control our own lands. Our women even walked around bare chested showing of their beautiful black breast not as a sex symbol to men, but as a way of being. The women did this until the white devil came along, and made it seem wrong. As we go back the Alpha in bible the snake Satan tricked Adam, and Eve into thinking nudity was an impurity, and abnormal the white devils did the same to us. Every black brother, and sister in the divine area right now hug one another, as a form of undying love unity for your black brothers, and sisters" Will said to the Black Nationals as they all stood at attention dressed in all black unlocking their hands from behind their backs to tightly hug one another listening vividly to Will as he continued to preach.....

Overtime the Black National's membership slightly grew, as the Black Nationals terror of vicious hate crimes dramatically increased.....

One late cold winter's night Ruby ran up to an parked squad car occupied by two white officer's with her coat open, and her shirt slighty torn with her big beautiful brown breast bouncing.....

"He tried to rape me, he tried to rape me," Ruby said to the officers.....

The officer was so mesmerized by the sight of those big ole titties, that they wasn't able to respond right back it was as they were in a trance.....

Within no time the officer's came back to reality.....

Both officer's got out of the car.....

"Who tried to rape you," one officer asked with his eyes on her breast. "Where he at," the other officer asked with his eyes stuck on her breast. "He in this alley," Ruby said.....

Ruby ran back to the alley as the police got in the squad car to follow her.

As they made it to the part of the alley were Ruby was at they wondered why she didn't get in the car with them instead of running back to the alley on her own.

They rushed out of their car before they could say a word Ruby sprayed them in the face with Mace. Then she begin cutting one in the face back to back, as he grabbed his gun busting shots unable to see due to the Mace in his eye he accidently shot his partner in the eye twice. The bullets went to his brain instantly leaving him for dead.

The Mace in the officer's eyes made him feel as if he was blind, as Ruby stabbed in his throat a few times he dropped his gun, as he himself collapsed to the ground Ruby got on top of him stabbing in both his eyes, his face, and his head, as he squealed like a pig, Ruby snatched his life away from him.....

After the short period of drama Ruby vanished away from the scene of the crime.....

Ruby was a member of the Black Nationals, she was thoroughbred, had more heart then most of the members in the Black Nationals, and she knew how to do her dirt smart, and kept her mouth shut.....

Days later Ruby walked up to some of the Black National members as they were discussing the two police getting killed. Never in their wildest dreams would they have imagined that Ruby was the one who killed the two police.....

Didn't nobody know what Ruby did, she had learned from Will to do dirt, and to keep your mouth close, that way you wouldn't have to worry about no one telling the police.....

Sometimes members of the Black Nationals would do dirt to white people by themselves, and keep their dirt to themselves; other times they'd get together in numbers to do dirt, they called it war games.....

One late quiet night Will, Black, Ruby, and two other members of Black National, Dennis, and Tody, all decided to play war games.

Sometimes they'd split up to play war games. This time they decided to do it together, but in two different cars that would be right behind one another.

They'd use the woman as driver's so that way after they did their dirt the men could duck down in the cars as if the women were in the car driving by themselves; that way it would be less likely the police to bother a car only occupied by one woman.

Will, Black, and Ruby was in one car. Tody, and Dennis trailed behind them in their car.....

While driving on a quiet side street unexpectedly they spotted a black prostitute just finished performing hardcore erotica for a white trick in a white Sedan. Black whom was sitting in the back seat of the first car signaled Todie, and Dennis to pull over.

Both cars pulled over on the other side of the street a short distance from the white trick in the sedan, and cut their lights off swiftly. The prostitute exited the car, and walked swiftly anxious to spend her earned money on buying her some dope.

He was so mesmerized by the sexual experience he just had with the prostitute that he sat in the car smoking a cancer stick oblivious to his surroundings and what was soon to come.....

Outta nowhere three shots sounded off like canons, "dooock, dooock, dooock." One bullet hit the white trick in the bottom part of the back of his head the other two hit him in his back.

Will felt wonderful after he shot the man up three times, as he ran back to the car the sounds of victorious trumpets sounded off in his head.....

As Will made it to the car all three men in both cars duck down, as the ladies smoothly coasted off as if nothing never happen the way Will taught them how to do it.....

"Did you get him, did you kill him," Ruby asked excitedly? Will begin slightly laughing. "I don't know I hope so," Will said.

About an hour later they found another victim. A white guy dressed up in a three piece suit walking down the street as if he owned the street with a briefcase in his hand.....

They pulled both cars around the corner Will got out and walked up to the man. As Will approached him the white gentleman looked up at Will with a smile upon his face on verge of greeting him. Will upped on him hitting him three times in the forehead the bullets ripped through his skull pushing half of his head off. The sight off it made Will so happy.

Will ran back to the cars jumping for joy.....

What Will didn't know was that the man he had killed was a homicide detective whom was coming home from work. Thw detective decided to walk home from work instead of driving, because his head was clouded by the constant murders, and secretive racism that was going on in his precinct, and around the world in general. The detective was on his way home to be with his black wife, and his two bi-racial kids.....

Later that night both car loads were mad, and jealous that Will had did all the killings himself that night. It was almost daybreak, and they had decided to call it a night. Ruby spotted this older white guy standing a bus stop on a main street.

She pleaded with Will to let her kill him. Will told her no the women were only used in war games to assist the men to get away. Ruby debated with Will that men, and women should be as equals especially the black men, and women. Although Ruby, and Will only debated for a short period of time Will decided to let her free to commit murder.

Both cars pulled around the corner, and parked, Will handt Ruby the gun, and told her to be careful. Once Ruby got out of the car Tody, and Dennis looked at her stun with no clue of what was going on.

As Ruby started to walk to her destination Will got out the car, and told Tody, and Dennis that Ruby was getting to kill the white chump at the bus stop.....

As soon as Will got back in his car, and slammed the door he heard six shots go off. The shots was so loud that it was if the were coming from only a few feet from him.....

Ruby had walked up to the white guy on the bus stop, and asked for a cigarette the white guy made a racial slur, as Ruby upped on him shot him up six times unloading her .38 revolver as the bullets ripped through his flesh she knew he wouldn't live through tips of hallows to see a better day tomorrow.....

In no time Ruby made her way back to the car got in the driver's side, and smoothly coasted off.....

As they drove away to their secret hide away they all visioned Ruby taking away that white chumps life.....

Right then, and there Will knew Ruby was a winner, and a proud member of Black National's.....

Overtime Will wondered, and wondered how would it be possible for his dream of Black Nationlism to come to reality. He wondered how would blacks begin to govern politics in their own communities, how would blacks become more book smart through education, and how would their be more blacks becomming business owners.....

Will, Black, amongst others in the Black National worked for the white men. And those that didn't work for the white men were either mechanics or beauticians whom didn't have their own shops yet. But all of the Black Nationals had one thing in common they all long for the day to come were they all lived like kings, and queens on earth legitimately without any crimimal grinding.....

"Black beauty's I'd like to thank each, and every one of you for showing up today it's my privilege to be part of this organization. Since we first started it's been all talk, and not enough action. We gotta figure out a way for improvement," Will said as everyone started to clapping, and cheering.....

Everyone started clapping and cheering because they'd been feeling the same way.....

Within the next meeting Will had came up with a plan to make black people slightly advance. He told them that were mechanics, and beautician to train other blacks those trades; not just the blacks in Black National, but black people in general. Will told them to do that so that they would be able to make extra money outside of their day jobs, and eventually be able to take their trade and earned money, and be able to open up small shops. Will also told the Black Nationals to go to libraries, and attend college to study politics, that way they'd be able to slightly advance on a political level. The Black Nationals followed instructions.....

Within only weeks Will would talk to members of Black National, and he could tell by their conversations that they'd followed orders. Will felt good that he planted mental seeds of growth that was slowly starting to grow.....

Over time the Black Nationals continued to play war games. The war games had slowed down dramatically, most of Black

National was more interested in the knowledge of being book smart......

Ruby, and Will feel in love with war games, most of the time when they played them it would be just them two......

One night after playing war games Will, and Ruby decided to go over his house to spend a night simply because it was late, and both of them were to sleepy to drive far. Will lived closer to where they was at than Ruby did so that's why they decided to go to his house. It was cool because Ruby's husband was a part of Black National, and Wallace's girlfriend whom didn't live with him was real cool with Ruby, and her husband......

Once they almost made it to Will's house it started to rain. When they made to Will's place they couldn't find a park therefore they had to park all the way up the street, and get out and run to his house in the rain in which left they close all wet up......

"You can go in my bedroom, and look in the closet my girlfriend left some clothes of hers in there, you can get a pair of her clothes, get in the shower, and change clothes. You can sleep in my bedroom I'll just sleep on the couch," Will said......

Will sat the couch feeling uncomfortable because of the wet clothes, and because he was fighting his sleep he wanted to wait until Ruby was done so he could get in the shower......

Within a few minutes Ruby came out the bathroom ass hole naked with only a towel drying off her hair.

Will stood to attention looking at Ruby as if he'd just seen a ghost......

"Ruby what are you doing," Will asked? "I'm drying my hair," she said calmly, and innocently. "Ruby where your clothes at," Will asked? "They're in the bathroom. I remembered what you had said at a meeting one time that we were free to walk around naked in Africa before the white man came, and poisioned our minds," Ruby said.

Their stood this naked beautiful black young lady. She stood five feet, chocolate super thick with such a cute face, and naturally curly hair......

This girl on some bullshit, she know she married to one of our black brothers, and she want to put me in this situation, Will thought to himself.....

She stopped drying her hair off dropped the towel on the floor and walked up to Will, and gently hugged him around his waist, as he didn't attempt to reject. She looked him in his eyes and told him,"I love you." "But you're married," he said. "But I'm only human, and I love you, and I want you take me as your queen, and do whatever you want to me, I belong to you," she said.

Will begin smiling, and laughing right before their lips connected, as they began playing the French kissing game that seemed like forever.....

Eventually Ruby snatched her lips away from his and fell to her knees. She looked up at him, and asked him,"can I suck your dick." "Go ahead," he said.

Ruby eagerly broke the button off his pants, and then unzipped them.

Once she pulled his dick out of his underwear she paused speechless she couldn't believe how long, and fat his dick was, she had never seen or had a dick that big.....

She wrapped her left hand around the back of the dick, then she tried putting it in her mouth she almost couldn't open her mouth wide enough to put it in but she finally did.

She stroked the back of his dick with her left hand as she ate his dick up as if she was hungry craving for it. She was sucking it vigoursly as if she was trying to suck the skin off of it, and shove it down her throat, and stroking it with her hand, all at the same damn time.

I love Ruby, I hope she never stop sucking my dick, Will thought to himself. At that instant moment she stopped took her mouth off his dick, and spit on his dick five times. Will couldn't believe she had just spit on him. She immediately started back sucking his dick. Will immediately felt how better it was after the moisture of the spit. Within seconds she paused and spit on his dick three more times back to back. Once she started back sucking on it the spit ran down her face which made her look like a sick dog foaming at the mouth.....

In no time flat Will was unleashing nut in her mouth as she drunk, and swallowed all of it like a champ.....

Afterwars Ruby laid on the couch on her back with her eyes shut thinking to herself like this guy getting ready to kill this pussy with that big ass dick, and he did just that.....

Will had her hollering, and screaming half the night. Before the night was done he even bust her the ass.....

After that night they promise not to let their sex interfere with their personal lives.....

# Chapter 2

Black entered Will's home.....
"Guess what happened," Black said. "What happened," Will asked? "I've been drafted to go fight in nam," Black said. Will paused, he couldn't believe what his ears were hearing.....

"That's sad," Will said in low tone of voice.

"Everything when been through, all the efforts we put forth to be black powerful superior to the devils, and they pulled this stunt.They don't want to treat us as equals but now they want you to fight their war," Will said. "I aint going Imma skip town," Black said. "You can't skip town, that's a case, you gone to have to do a prison term when they catch up with you, that's a federal case I think they call it draft dodging or something like that," Will said. "So what would you do if they drafted you for war," Black asked? "I don't know, that's a good question. I might just go and kill up some of them Orientals. I think I'd rather try my luck on the battle field, than spend a long term in prison," Will said.....

Will, and Black paused for a moment in time as their minds was flooded with alot of unanswered questions, as they visualized the battle fields in Vietnam, death and destruction, and the past history of the white men hate, instead of loving.....

Within the upcoming days Black decided to go to fight the war in Vietnam.....

"Good evening my black, and beautiful people," Will said to the Black National Organization. "Good evening," the Black National Organization said back to Will simultaneously.....

"We were all design, and taught to be warriors to live, eat, and breed, on a militant mind settings, we have military minds. That comes from ancient African tribes that's the way we survived and ruled our lands as soilders of war. Right now the white man has his own personal war going on, and forces us to fight it, due to their laws we have no other choice if called upon. No matter what happens don't let the white people tear you down mentally nor physically. Stick your chest out, and hold your head up, and concur all obstacles.....To the devils we are ugly to me we're all black, and beautiful," Will said full-heartedly.....After that meeting the Black Nationals begin to think more about the art of war.....

A couple weeks later Black was shipped of to Vietnam nervous, and worried about if he'll make it through alive. At this time Black was only twenty one years old, Will was only twenty years old, Ruby was twenty three. Majority of the Black Nationals were young, but they had the brains of people twice their age.....

Will decided to quit his job working for the white man. He felt as if he should practice what he preach. Will knew how to cut hair so he started cutting hair, as a hustle, and it paid of instantly.....

---

Once Black first made it to war he noticed that the soilders had to do extreme workouts. And he knew that his turn on the battle field was soon to come.....

After a period of training Black was sent to the battle field for war. He was nervous like never before in life, but he didn't let it show.

During his first few times on the battle fields he was lucky they didn't come across any enemy troops.....

His first time coming across enemy troops was one late night as the mosquitos constantly ate away at the soilders flesh as the hot dreary night seemed endlessly they walked across dry land as Black, as well as the other soilders hoped that they didn't step on a land mind which would be a painful death they made it to a small body of water which was only approximately two feet high.

They crossed the water, and made it these short bushes. As they stood still in the water in which seperated them from dry land they looked in them, and seen a small camp of enemy troops.

The general gave signal with his hand for everyone to remain silent. Then the general used his fingers as sign language giving orders in the way to attack.....

Black became even more nervous each second. He knew it was time for war, time to seperate the boys from the man.....

In no time the soilders were attacking enemy troops the sounds of on going rapid gun fire that flooded the sound waves of ears as grenades sounded off like rocket launchers. You could hear crying, screaming, yelling in different languages as death, and destructions became one.....

Once that battle was over the U.S stood triumphant, their was casulties of war on both sides. Majority of the casulties was that of the enemy troops. Those that the U.S. didn't put to death fled the camp.....

That night Black seen how prosperous the art of surprise could be......

Overtime Black experienced more episodes of being front line on the battle field, as soilders were constantly getting killed, Black started to like war fair.....

Overtime the other soilders begin to call Black, God. They nicknamed him God because everytime they'd go onto the battle field it seemed as if he had God on his side.....

Will, and Black stayed in constant contact mainly through letters, occasionally over the phone they'd talk.....

Black would tell Will how intense the war in nam was, and that it made their war games seem like a joke. Will told Black that the Black National were starting to rotate with the ViceLords. Black didn't like it, Black knew the ViceLords was a street gang.....

Will had met some of the outstanding members of ViceLords by cutting hair. Will had came to find out that they had some of the same exact concepts that Black Nationals had. They were even getting funded from the goverment to help uplift the black community, as a sign of thanks and reparation for blacks helping building this country which was long overdue.....

Will had been introduced to the minister of ViceLords. The minister instantly took a liking for Will because he was smart, and he showed the qualities of a leader.....

Overtime Will had did alotta dirt for the minister, Will would bring nightmares of death, and blood shed to reality for the minister.....

Within time Will, and majority of the Black Nationals became ViceLords, the minister made Will a five star universal elite.....

The king of ViceLord kept hearing good things about Will, and decided to start rotating with him a little. The king didn't rotate with to many people heavy; He loved people, but didn't trust no one.....

The king of ViceLord rotating with Will a little turned into alot. The king had never met someone so young, so thorough, and so dedicated to the upliftment of ViceLord, and the upliftment of the black community.....

At this point in time the ViceLords wasn't very deep but they we're on fast uprise. The mainly resided on the west of Chicago. Their were a few in the surrounding suburbs, but they wasn't that deep.....

Will would go out, and do recruiting, and go out and provide knowledge, and finance, and whatever assistance he could to the black community.....

In no time flat Will was a supreme elite, and had jurisdiction to create gang literature that the ViceLords had to abide by. He also had the kings blessings to start his own branch of ViceLord if he decided he wanted to do that.....

Will worked on the literarure of ViceLord with the king, and the minister, and now had expectations in becomming the king of his own branch of Vicelord.....

Within the matter of months Will finally decided to start his own branch of ViceLord, his branch would be the Traveler ViceLords, T.V.L.....

Mainly but not all branches of ViceLord name derived from ancient African tribes.

The Traveler tribe was an ancient tribe from Africa that traveled to conquer other tribes but not in war, but using their brains to manipulate them to became as one. The traveler tribe would find out were slave ship were and go to kill white slave traders, sometimes they'd became successful, other times they'd come up unsuccessful slaughtered like animals, but those that would survive would continue on, on their missions.....

Their were many other ancient African tribes; the Mandego's, the Zulu's, the Shabazz, the Ghosts, but Will decided to use the Travelers name because they were more in the likeness of himself, and his beliefs.....

Will became the youngest king of any branch of ViceLord that ever existed.....

# Chapter 3

After a year, and a half fighting in Vietnam Black's tour of duty was over, he was sent back home. He couldn't wait to touch the city streets again.....

Will went to pick up Black from the airport in one of his new cars. As they drove, and reminisced Will took Black through the areas were ViceLords dwelled Black was impresses.

Will took Black through the areas were they Travelers was, and Black couldn't believe how Will had blossomed in the streets while he was gone.

Black was impressed by Will's street growth, but still had the Black National concept embedded in his mind frame in which he didn't believe in Will's committing crimes.....

As the day turned to night Will took Black through one of his spots were they sold his dope at.

The spot was inside a small building, the dope fiends would go into the front door, and walk shortly to a door with a slot in it where the mail man would stick their mail in. The dope fiends would slide their money through that slot, and tell the people on the other side of the door exactly how many bags of dope they were interested in purchasing.

Will had someone in the front of the building on security so when the police come they could get rid of all the drugs, the money, and the gun. They'd get rid of it by quickly taking front part of their vent off, and giving it to the neighbors, or they would just give it to one of the neighbors up stairs; the upstairs neighbors would drop a long cord down for them to load up their merchandise in when, and if the police ever came.....

Will, and Black sat across the street on top of the hood of Will's car checking out the business. Black couldn't believe how many customers were constantly coming, and how much money Will had to be making off all them customers.....

Many of the Black Nationals became Travelers. Those they didn't become Traveler still did things to uplift the black people in their on way, and time.

The Black Nationals never told anyone, about their involvement with Black National, or the war games they played. They all kept it secret, they didn't even tell the Travelers that wasn't initially Black Nationals, about Black Nationals.

From time to time the ex-Black Nationals continued to play war games.....

After they left Will dope spot they went to see all of the ex-Black Nationals. All of them was more than happy to see Black home from the war.....

The last ex-Black National member they went to see was Ruby. Tears of joy ran down Ruby's face; she was so happy that he made it home safe, because so many people was getting killed in that war.....

Will ended up dropping Black off at his moms house, and went to meet Ruby at his own house.....

Will went, and jumped in the shower, as Ruby sat on the couch with the tip of her finger in her mouth, sucking on it as if she was a shy teenage girl.

Will came out of the bathroom wearing a robe.

As Will robe dropped to the ground Ruby took off her dress in which she had no panties, no bra. She dropped to her knees, with purple lipstick on she gently placed Will's dick in her mouth begin humming and bobbing back, and forth doing her best to make him fill pleasure, and love through the art of dick sucking.....

Ruby, and Will had got real close, but they kept their loving a secret. Ruby loved Will as if was he an angel on earth. Will loved Ruby, adored her sex, but loved his real girlfriend even more.....

They next morning Will went to go pick up Black. Will took Black shopping for clothes, and took him to the car lot, and brought him a brand new Cadillac.....

As Black started driving the area in his new lac with Will in the passenger seat a dude named Smurf spotted them, and flagged them down. As they parked Smurf ran to the passenger seat, and Black easily raised down the window.....

"William, Dirt robbed me," Smurf said. "Don't never call me William, call me Will. My Dirt, Traveler Dirt robbed you," Will said. "Yep, he robbed me last night, I was looking for you all night, you was no where to be found. I was gone took care of my business, but I can't bring no hurt, harm, or danger to one of the ViceLord brothers, that's just like doing something to one of my family members," Smurf said. "How much he rob you for," Will asked? "A bill, and a quarter," Smurf said. "One, twenty-five," Will said, and then reached in his pocket pulled out a roll of money, counted out a hundred, and twenty five dollars, and gave it to Smurf.

"That's good the way you went about the situation. By us being black men, and ViceLords all of us are like family, well atleast we suppose to be like family. But T.V.L. is like my immediate family. Like I just said it's good that you went about it the way you did, 'cause if you ever cross me, and do something to anybody claiming T.V.L. it's gonna be killer clowns, guns that explode, and burning of eternal fire all at once as a rapture you must feel," Will said. "Come on William, I meant to say Will you know I wouldn't never do nothing to none of the Travelers," Smurf said. "I heard that slick shit you said out your mouth, talking about you was gonna handle your business. As long as I'm living, and breathing you or nobody else aint gone do shit to no Traveler, and if you do you aint gone get away with, so don't let me hear nothing like that come out your mouth again. Just meet me in the pool hall tomorrow around twelve thirty,or one, we gone enforce law on dirt," Will said. "Alright, I'll be there," Smurf said as he stepped away from the car, as Black pulled off.....

"I been knowing you for umteen years, and you make everybody call you Will. Whats wrong with calling you William, thats your full name," Black said. "Yes, you have known me for umteen years, and you been calling me Will for umteen years so just stick with it," Will said. "Well from now on call me God," Black said. "I'm not calling no other man God," Will said. "That's my name, they gave me that name while I was at war. They gave me that name because each time I'd go to battle I'd always stand triumphant, and I'd always make it back safe," Black said. "Okay then God," Will said possessing a big smile on his face.....

The next morning Will, God, and some of the ViceLords were in the pool hall shooting pool. Some where smoking cigars, while others were sipping cheap wine, while others were doing both. Will, didn't smoke or drink.....

While shooting pool Will kept looking out of the window to across the street. Will had a dime bag powder spot across the street. He kept looking over there observing the customers in, and out the indoor spot.....

Will winding up sending someone to get Dirt.....

About an hour later in comes Dirt through the pool hair door with one of the other Lords by his left side.....

"Will you was looking for me," Dirt said, as everyone in the pool hall stopped what they was doing, and got quiet.

Before Will answered Dirt, Dirt noticed Smurf standing over in the cut. Dirt immediately put his hand on his gun which was tucked in the waist of his pants. Then he gave Smurf a mean mugg, a cold stare, that of a villing from a nightmare.

Reality immediately came forth Dirt now knew what Will had wanted him for.

Although Dirt wasn't at all worried about Smurf pulling a stunt in the presence of Will he still clutched his gun just to let Smurf know if he got out of his body he'd be feeling the pain of bullets.....

Dirt step closer to Will as everyone including Smurf surrounded him.....

"This brother said you robbed him," Will said to Dirt. "Yeah I robbed him so what he aint no Traveler, he a Renegade, fuck 'em," Dirt said.....

All the other ViceLords that wasn't Travelers, and those that was frowned up in disgust.

"So what he aint he aint no Traveler, he still a ViceLord. That's why I be telling ya'll to learn ya'll lit, then ya'll will know how to conduct ya'll self as ViceLords. Now if this brother would've came back and did something to you the Travelers would've had to murder the Renegades making them extinct going against the laws, and policies of ViceLords, and killing of our own black brothers," Will said as everyone remained speechless.....

"You gotta learn your lit, you in violation for baring arms against a member of ViceLord, disobeying the laws of ViceLord unity, and jeopardizing the body of ViceLord. Normally you suppose to get a minute for each charge, but by this being you first time in violation you gone get one minute from head to toe. Big C collect all the weapons from all the brothers in this room," Will said.

Big C was a Conservative ViceLord. Always at meetings, or when a brother was in violation there was to be no weapons, because meetings, and violations were considered to be somewhat spiritual, and uplifting.....

Once Big C collected all the weapons from the brothers they all tucked in their shirts faced the east, bowed their heads closing their eyes, lifting their palms up.....

God stood in the cut watching everything amazed about how the ViceLords orchestrated things.....

Big C started to read the Statement of Love, "For you my brother my love begins at birth that has manifested itself throughout our heritage for the color of our skin which is black. For I am you, you are me. Our minds are for the same cause. Our efforts are for the same goals. Our souls bound for the same destination. Our lives are for the same new nation. For you my black brother I give my unity, my vitality, my undying love, almighty."

Once Big C was done reading the statement they all opened their eyes, and lifted their heads up.

Dirt stood against the wall.

Will looked at his watch then in a matter of seconds he gave Big C the go ahead, to violate Dirt.

Big C hit dirt in the face once, Dirt fell to the floor as Big C continued violating him for a minute.

After the violation Dirt stood to his feet body aching in slight pain, he shook each ViceLord hand, and then hugged them.

He shook, and hugged Will last. As he hugged Will, Will whispered in his ear, "learn your lit."

Afterwards Dirt, and the guy he came in the pool hall with left, and everybody started back playing pool, smoking, drinking, and laughing as if nothing never happen.....

God started to fall in love with the way the ViceLords did things.....

Will and God left the pool hall.....

"That was raw the way you did things back there, what was that, that guy was reading," God asked? "That was the Statement of Love, that a piece of ViceLord literature, I'm the one that wrote it. Alot of ViceLord literature I wrote. I took alot of Black Nationals concept, and turned them into ViceLord concepts, and wrote it up in literature. Me or none of the others that was once Black National told the ViceLords about the Black National, I'll take that secret to the grave with me," Will said. "Literature I didn't even know gangs had literature," God said. "We not actually gang we're a nation of people that's about the upliftment of black people. ViceLord is design to uplift the black people," Will said.....

God stopped at a stop sign and pulled out a cigarette, and set fire to it, and begin puffing.....

"You smoke cigarettes, you digging yourself an early grave. Black Nationals, are not to use drugs, alcohol, or smoke tobacco," Will said. "Black Nationals, don't suppose to commit crimes, unless they were hate crimes," God said, and then inhaled, and exhaled cigarette smoke. "But I commit crimes, for the uplifting of the community. I sell alotta drugs, but I take the money, and invest it into good things within the black community," Will said. "You tearing down the black community, selling them drugs," God said. "But if I don't sell it to them it's many others that will. But I promise you majority of my money is being invested into positive things that will make blacks prosperous in the future," Will said.....

Within the upcoming weeks God noticed that Will was serious, because he seen with own eyes how Will helped black with the money he made of drugs. Will would give black churches large sums of money,provided blacks with places to live outside of the ghetto, help people with their bills, and donate money to schools for better, advanced books, so blacks could get a higher learning.....

God start to see with his own eyes how the goverment would help fund ViceLord; and that the ViceLord would do many things for the black community, such as help blacks find jobs, provide after school programs so that the kids could come there to study, and have fun, amongst other things.....

God started to spend time with ex-Black Nationals that had become Travelers he noticed that none of them were in the streets selling drugs, or committing crimes they were working in places of after school programs, drug treatment centers in the black community or in college working on degrees.....

In no time God became a Traveler. He went from having no status to a branch elite, that dictated only to Traveler ViceLords, to a universal elite that dictated to all Vicelords, then to the prince of T.V.L. And he earned his way up to that title......

The Traveler ViceLords, amongst other branches of ViceLords rapidly grew, and spreaded throughout the city, and to the surrounding suburbs.....

God started apply his military experience in Vietnam to the ViceLord structure. In the military when soilders were punished for minor things they'd only have to do a harsh workout. God put within ViceLord law that if a representitive of ViceLord did something minor to break law they wouldn't have to get violated physically, but they would only have to do a harsh work out. The king of all ViceLords, and the minister liked that concept.....

# Chapter 4

O nce Dr. Martin Luther King was killed the streets was filled with rage. Will, and God came up with notion that if the ViceLords wanted to commit hate crimes against white people than go ahead, but ViceLords were not to burn down business, and buildings in the black community, no matter if a white person owned them or not. The king of all ViceLords, and the ministers, and supreme elites of other branches of ViceLord shared this notion, and told ViceLord not to tear down the black community by destroying business, and buildings in the black community, no matter if a white person owned them or not.....

Although most of the ViceLords obeyed the orders it didn't matter because black gangs, and those that wasn't gang affiliated tore the city up......

Shortly after Dr. Martin Luther King Jr. was killed the ViceLord amongst other gangs had stopped getting funds for the goverment. The goverment claimed they were embezzling funds. So now drug dealings and black, and black crimes instantly started to reach an all time high.....

The original king of ViceLords, and the minister step back, and let the supreme elites govern the mob; they step down because they were being investigated by the feds.

The entire ViceLord nation became more needy of Will, and God's leadership.....

Will, and God started to open up more dope spots so they could use the money to fund growth, and development of the black community.....

With their owned dope money they were able to keep open some of the drug rehibilatation centers, and a couple of the centers that helped blacks get jobs amongst other things.....

Will, and God opened up with dope in the projects that made them start to see more money than they had ever did before in their lives; the projects was a gold mind.....

Since the Renegades was the deepest branch of ViceLord in the projects they started going through Smurf to sell their dope, Smurf was a three star universal elite.....

As the money grew more, and more people wanted to become T.V.L.

Smurf, and majority of the Renegades ended up flipping T.V.L. It was good for them, because they was still ViceLords just a different branch. Will made Smurf a five star universal elite.....

Daily more, and more of all branches of ViceLord depending on Will, God, or some of the other travelers for assistance, and guidance, and Travelers extended their hand, as a sign of love, and support.

More, and more the Traveler mob grew. Other people that were from different branches ViceLord started to flip Traveler, as well as oppositons wanted to be part of T.V.L., and even those that wasn't gang affiliated became T.V.L.

Other gangs in the city forced people to become members, or forced oppositons to flip. The Travelers, and the other branches of ViceLord didn't, people wanted to be down 'cause the ViceLords were thoroughbred.....

Within time ViceLords everywhere honored King Will, as the King of Kings.....

# Chapter 5

Will, and God started to have problems out of their main girlfriends, more, and more their main girlfriends wanted more time together, instead of space; they'd often be questioned about creeping with other women; one time God's main chick even threw his clothes out on the front porch, and poured bleach, and paint all over them.....

Will, and Ruby decided to take a trip to Indiana to rotate with some people to attempt to lay down a foundation for T.V.L. Ruby's husband told her while she was in Indiana he'll be leaving the state as well to go visit a sick, dying family member.....

God drove Ruby, and Will to the airport. Right before Ruby, and Will got out of the car Ruby gave God the keys to her house told him that her husband would be out of town, and that she had forgot to call an electrician, and then asked him if he could go over her house to do some electrical work. He gladly accepted the keys, and said yes.....

God learned how to do electrical work when he was younger, from his uncle.....

The next day God went to Ruby's house, as soon as he stepped a foot in the door he could see clouds of smoke, as if the inside of the house was slightly on fire as he smelled the reefer smoke he paused for a fifteen seconds not even closing the door behind himself, but loving the smell of burning reefer, and wanting to smoke some of it.....

God stepped in the house closed the door, and locked it. Walked to the bedroom, and there Ruby's husband was giving some lady's pussy all of his dick in the rawest form.....

Ruby's husband was on top of this lady, as she had her legs on his shoulder choking her neck with both of her hands as if he was really trying to choke her to death slamming his dick all the way in, and out of her pussy as if he was mad at the world, she moaned, and pleaded with him, "stop, stop, don't, no, no." As Ruby husband kept giving her the dick God became pleased with the action. Ruby's husband begin slamming his dick in her pussy harder and faster as his grip around her neck became firmer his nut exploded within her pussy. At that very it was as God could actually feel the intense pleasure that Ruby's husband had acheived.

Ruby's husband, and the lady didn't know God was slightly in the room with them, they was to busy fucking.

As Ruby's husband finished nutting, God seen the woman's face.

Damn Ruby's husband fucking Will's main girl Thunder, God thought to himself as he quickly vanished out of the room.....

God left the room, but stood to a distance where he could still see the action, but they couldn't see him unless they got up, and looked directly that way, and even if they did look that way he'd try to move swiftly so they would'nt see him.....

Ruby's husband took his dick out of her pussy, grabbed a little tube out of his pants pocket that was on the floor. The tube had raw cocaine in it. He opened the tube sprinkled cocaine on both of her titties nipples, then snorted it off. Then he put a little cocaine on his tongue, and went down, and started eating her pussy as she laid there on the bed loving every second of it.....

Once he stopped eating her pussy, she stayed laying on the bed, he began fucking her mouth like it was actual pussy, feeding her the dick, and choking her with it.....

What God didn't know was that she loved being choked while having sex, rather it was hands around her neck, or with a dick.....

God rushed out of the house closing the front door behind himself, but making a mistake, and leaving it unlock.....

God left not knowing what to do. He couldn't tell Will what he seen Will loved Thunder, and Ruby loved her husband; and also God knew that Will was creeping of with Ruby although he never caught them in the act it was still obvious.

Thunder, and Ruby's husband started creeping 'cause they both new that Will, and Ruby was creeping although they was never caught in the act it was still obvious, because they spent to much time together.....

Once Will, and Ruby came back from Indiana God was there to pick them up from the airport.....

God immediately told Ruby that he didn't get a chance to go over her house to do the electrical work, she told him no problem she'd just call an electrician.....

Excitedly Will told God about the ViceLords that he had rotated with in Indiana, and that they wanted to become Traveler ViceLords, instead of Conservatives, and they had potentials on pushing alot of dope, weed, and cocaine for him so that he could now help the black community in Indiana. All the while, while Will talk all God could think about was Ruby's husband slamming his dick in and out of Thunder. God decided to keep what he'd seen a secret although he wanted to tell his right hand man Will, about Thunder.....

God dropped Ruby off at home. Then him, and Will went over to Will's house.....

Will came out the kitchen eating a sandwich drinking on a pop out the bottle, and seen God on the couch looking like he was getting ready to fall asleep.

"Why is you always so sleepy all the time," Will asked God? "I been up all night fucking around with this new chick, the one I was telling you about from out south. The bitch got a mouth piece that's, that of another planet. I been smoking reefer to that's what got me a little sleepy," God said. "You need to stop smoking reefer, and cigarettes, it's no good for, that's what I miss about Black National we was against all that," Will said. "I'm T.V.L., don't get me wrong Black National gone always be in my heart, but I'm T.V.L.," God said. "I wish I could of put no drug usage in

ViceLord lit, I could but I know it'll never work, to many of our black brothers, and sisters love to get high, that's why I can't til the day come when I don't got to sell drugs to our black brothers, and sisters, when I have enough money to retire from the drug game, and focus on rebuilding, and uplifting the blacks. Although I'm T.v.L. til the death of me Imma always have Black Nationalism in my heart," Will said, and finished the last of his sandwich, and sip of pop.....

"I'm getting ready to shit, shower, and shave, and go to sleep. Once I wake we gone go check on Smurf to see what the projects been doing. Did you check on the other spots while I was gone," Will asked? "Yeah, I only got seventy six thousand, and few odd hundreds the few days you was gone," God said. "Only seventy six thousand, you said that like it aint nothing," Will said. "It aint nothing compared to what we usually get in a few days," God said. "Yeah you right about that. But that's cool I can re-up, and still have enough to put some money into the blacks after school programs, and re-habs center," Will center. "You are a good brother, and it's good that you do what you can to uplift the black community, but that's not normal for a guy to sell all that dope to blacks, and then open re-hab centers for blacks," God said. "Yeah I know right, it's my only hope, the only answer to my prayers to uplift the black community. That's the only way a black guy like me can get so much money, so fast to use to uplift our black brothers, and sisters. As God, not you the real God is my witness if everything go as plan I'm done selling dope, or doing any criminal activities. Imma be so rich that I can spend all my money, and time bringing forth a change in black community. But when it's all said, and done Imma be Black National, and T.V.L. to I reach Heaven or Hell," Will said, as he walked away from God, going to the bathroom to shit, shower, and shave.....

Once Will shitted, shaved, and shower he went and looked at God laid out on the couch sleep. He walked over to God and slighty lifted the sleeve of his right arm that showed the marks on his arm.....

This guy is the co-founder of Black National, and the prince of Travelers everywhere and a straight dopefiend. How he think that I don't know he shoot dope with all them marks oh his arms always trying to cover his arm up with all them long sleeve shirt, when it be hot as hell outside, always talking he been smoking reefer, you been shooting dope, Will that to himself.....

Once Will, and God finished sleeping they went to see Smurf.....

As they pulled up to the projects they seen a mass amount of dopefiends walking up, and pulling up to buy dope as the workers would tell them that they wasn't working. As soon as they parked their car in front of the building Smurf came running out of the building as if someone was chasing him and bailed in the backseat.....

"I been steady calling ya'll, we been out of dope since yesterday morning," Smurf said. "You sold all that dope that fast," Will said. "Yep the building been tipping, I think it's a drought on good dope," Smurf said. "It aint no drought, they just don't got a good connect like I do," Will said. "You need to start selling weight I gotta alotta people driving down on me trying to buy large pieces of dope. Some the Lords off the ave. trying to buy two-hundreds grams. We should start selling weight, we can start taxing people for our good dope," Smurf said. "Okay I'll front you a hundred grams to sell in weight," Will said. "How much I gotta bring you back," Smurf asked? "I don't know I'll give you a price later. Right now I'm all outta of dope, I been out a town wasn't able to re-up, but I'll make sure you get some work later on tonight. Imma send you those hundred grams, and Imma send fifty bundles, Imma turn the bundles into two thousand bundles, and put an extra bag in each pack for the workers can get an extra sawbuck. How much you owe me already, fifty five thousand right," Will asked? "Naw it's fifty six, when they brought the bundles they thought it was fifty five but it was fifty six somebody musta miscounted," Smurf said. "Alright thats cool, Imma send somebody to pick up the money and bring you the dope. A'ight get out I gotta go I'm in a hurry," Will said. "Take me right down the street so I can get me something to eat," Smurf said.....

What's taking this guy so long, Will thought to himself as Smurf finally came out the restaurant with his food in hand.....

Smurf got into the car slammed the door hard, ripped open the paper bag, and started eating. Will, and God looked him in digust.....

"Uhhh you eating that pork," God said. "I should get you violated, even if you do eat pork atleast don't do it around the brothers," Will said. "I eat, pussy, pork, jello pudding pops, and all type of shit. I snort dope shoot dope, and cocaine, shot people, and a bunch other shit. Don't get me wrong I do honor ViceLord law but I'm not trying to hear nothing about not eating pork," Smurf said. "You betta be trying to hear it before you get violated," Will said.....

They dropped Smurf off at the building and went their seperate ways.....